THE
ART of
LIVING
in
PEACE

THE ART of LIVING in PEACE

Towards a New Peace Consciousness

PIERRE WEIL

Findhorn Press

Original French text © UNESCO 1992
This English edition first published 1994

ISBN 0 905249 96 8

Cover by Posthouse Printing
based on a design by Patricia Andersson

Translation by Sandra Kramer with Thierry Bogliolo
Layout and setting in Avant Garde by Findhorn Press
Printed and bound by The Guernsey Press Ltd

Published by Findhorn Press, The Park, Findhorn,
Forres IV36 0TZ, Scotland

CONTENTS

Appendix 1

Appendix 2

Yes, never before during the last forty years has peace been so within reach of humanity, never has it been so palpable as today. Yes, peace is possible at all levels of life, and it is up to the human race to create peace or plunge into the horrors of war. Yes, today humanity is at the crossroads where it must choose peace with courage, determination and imagination.

For more than forty years Unesco has been working to establish peace in the human mind, as the constitution of Unesco states: 'Since wars begin in the minds of men, it is in the minds of men that the defences of peace must be constructed.'

Federico Mayor, Director General of Unesco, at the preliminary meeting to the Yamoussoukro Conference on Peace in the Minds of Men. Unesco, September 6, 1988.

The Art of Living in Peace Workshop

Although this book, *The Art of Living in Peace,* stands on its own as a reference for education for peace, it also holds the source material for the workshop of the same name, developed by Pierre Weil at the International Holistic University of Brasilia.

If you are interested in participating in the *Art of Living in Peace* workshop and would like more information about facilitators and venues, please contact:

Education Department
Findhorn Foundation
The Park
Findhorn
Forres IV36 0TZ
Scotland

PREFACE

On the threshold of the 21st century, humanity is confronted with a number of interrelated problems which constitute challenges for our very survival. We have to deal with crucial issues on equitable and sustainable development, protection of the environment, population questions and the promotion of democracy and respect for human rights. In view of the urgent need to find solutions to these major problems, would it not be justifiable to discuss universal values and new universal ethics? These could be called, for example, planetary ethics, world citizenship, global or holistic thinking, and would be based on humanistic and cultural values and on the realities concerning the survival of our planet and the maintenance of decent life, as well as recognising the necessity that all people should live together in peace with different cultural identities and backgrounds.

Within the United Nations system, Unesco is responsible for building the defences of peace in the minds of men in particular through education as it is emphasised in the Unesco Constitution (adopted in 1946). Forty-eight years later, this mission is still just as relevant. The world has experienced, and is still experiencing, many local and regional conflicts. We are again witnessing wars based on prejudices and the doctrine of inequality of people and races and their monstrous corollary of 'ethnic cleansing'. This proves, if proof is needed, that peace education is a long-term undertaking. Walls may have been pulled down but at the same time other conflicts have hardened elsewhere.

Peace education is also a challenge. Long-standing customs, habits, prejudices and traditions may inhibit many enthusiastic initiatives and may lead to problems when faced with different new customs and traditions. But we are encouraged to find ways of creating a new awareness and a more responsible form of citizenship towards a future of peace.

The Art of Living in Peace is the result of a seminar for teachers of teacher-training colleges organised by Unesco in order to promote the exchange of innovative experiments in international education, and Unesco would like to pay tribute to the author, Pierre Weil, Chairman of the City of Peace Foundation, International Holistic University of Brasilia, whose experience and untiring dedication and energy continue to contribute so greatly to the development of education for peace.   ·

The publication of *The Art of Living in Peace* by the Findhorn Foundation — well known in the world for its dynamism and conviction in creating peace, harmony and beauty on Earth in a holistic way — will undoubtedly represent a significant work in the field of peace education, showing that peace is a conquest, but not by force of arms.

Kaisa Savolainen
Director,
Section for Humanistic, Cultural
  and International Education
UNESCO

INTRODUCTION

The pursuit of peace is an exhilarating adventure. The congress therefore suggests a new programme that makes practical and effective provision for new visions and approaches in cooperation, education, science, culture and communication, taking into consideration the cultural traditions of different parts of the world.

Yamoussoukro Declaration on Peace in the Minds of Men. Unesco, July 26, 1989.

During the forty years' existence of the United Nations, and of Unesco in particular, a great deal of research has been carried out into the causes of war and the means to establish peace in the world.

All over the world, in parallel with this research, a curriculum for teaching peace is being developed, to a large extent inspired by the research and its conclusions as well as by the work and official statements of these international organisations.

The time has come to attempt to form an overview of this research and these teaching methods in order both to understand them intellectually and to trigger a profound change in the attitudes and behaviour of human beings.

A new consciousness is developing in the minds of many of our fellow human beings, together with a change of paradigm which inspires a new way of looking at science, philosophy, art and education. A new holistic vision of the world is in the process of being born.

It is important that educators for peace all over the world are aware of this development and its implications for all of us, and that this information is made available in language that is as simple and accessible as possible.

Moreover, for educators to be in tune with the times and to be able to respond to the demands of current events, we must provide them with the educational methods for transforming consciousness, starting with their own, so that they themselves can be examples of peace and harmony. Indeed, how can we change other people, if we do not start with ourselves?

MODULE 1
PRELIMINARY CONSIDERATIONS

This book is written in simple language that is easily understood by the main cultures on Earth and attempts to bring together theoretical data with recommended practical techniques that can be used in education for peace.

Therefore, each description of the conclusions drawn from hypotheses and research about peace, about the obstacles that prevent its realisation and the methods which encourage its development or awakening, is accompanied by methodological curriculum recommendations for short-, medium- and long-term education.

Short-term refers to a 15- to 20-hour programme, which allows participants to become aware of the problem. A prototype workshop of this kind has been initiated by the City of Peace Foundation and the International Holistic University of Brasilia, under the title *The Art of Living in Peace*. It serves as an introduction to a training programme for educators and teachers of peace, but also — and above all — it is meant for the general public all over the world and will be used during Unesco's regional seminars.

Medium-term refers to a 3- to 6-month programme which goes more deeply into the contents of the short-term workshop.

Long-term refers to a programme which provides an in-depth education in this art as it should be developed in all the schools of the world.

We consider that this type of education should begin with the educators themselves. By setting an example with their own inner peace and passing it on in their interactions with others, they will be able to go beyond the mere teaching of concepts that is typical of today's world.

Each part of this book may be considered as an educational module. For each module you will find:

- A summary of the principal aspects of the subject and the current situation.
- A reference list of essential sources. These lists are certainly not exhaustive, however, and each reference will lead the interested reader on to other works.
- A list of recommended educational methods.
- A short list of suggested reading.

Method of education

The contents of this programme are in line with the recommendations and, in particular, embody the spirit of the following documents issued by Unesco:

- The Preamble to Unesco's Constitution
- The Recommendation Concerning Education for International Understanding, Cooperation and Peace and Education Relating to Human Rights and Fundamental Freedoms, 1974.
- The Seville Statement on Violence, 1986.
- The Venice Declaration on Science and the Boundaries of Knowledge, 1987. Reinforced by the Vancouver Declaration, 1989.
- The Preparatory Meeting to the International Experts' Conference of Yamoussoukro on Peace in the Minds of Men, 1988.
- The Yamoussoukro Declaration on Peace in the Minds of Men, 1989.

As a method of education, we recommend alternating between theory and practical action in real life. We start with the theory in order to prepare people to absorb the real-life experience. After they have had the experience, we return to the theory and examine what has taken place, so that we can draw some conclusions or even make some decisions with regard to daily life. This also allows people to share their experiences with others taking the course.

The techniques employed are inspired by a variety of sources and cultures, and this in itself serves to increase international understanding. We would like to mention the following sources in particular:

- 'Active' methods of education from Europe.
- Explanatory methods common to all cultures.
- Dialectical methods as practised by all major cultures.
- Various types of yoga originating from India, Nepal and Tibet.
- T'ai-Chi as practised in China.
- Martial arts practised in Japan and China.
- Dance from all over the world.
- Music as a non-verbal international language.
- The graphic arts.
- Theatre and role-playing.
- Educational and traditional games.
- Mass media techniques and their educational role in the world: the press, radio, TV, advertising, propaganda.
- Training techniques used in the business world.
- Non-violent methods from India.
- Conflict management techniques originating from various European and American psychological and sociological schools of thought.
- Practices for awakening wisdom from African, Indian, shamanic, Jewish, Christian, Muslim, Hindu, Buddhist,

etc. traditions.

● Group and individual psychotherapy techniques.

While respecting the diversity of these sources, it is important to attempt gradually to develop a holistic, inter-disciplinary and transdisciplinary approach to education for peace. We shall return to this point later in the book.

We shall start with an introduction to the theoretical aspects of our programme. This is necessary since it under-lines the fact that a new paradigm is emerging, the impor-tance of becoming aware of it and its crucial influence on the development of a new approach to education for peace.

These preliminary thoughts will lead us to the heart of the matter: the aforementioned new method of educa-tion for peace — The Art of Living in Peace — inspired by one of the fundamental models developed by the Inter-national Holistic University of Brasilia.

The contents of the second part of the book are the result of twenty or so years of research on and refining of a method of awareness-awakening that had the primary objective of helping individuals find their own inner peace and its relation to certain states of consciousness. In addi-tion this method demonstrates how the reality in which we live is a function of our state of mind in any given moment. This research was carried out by the Department of Psy-chology at the Federal University of Minas Gerais, Brazil, under the auspices of the Chair of Transpersonal Psychol-ogy. We originally called this research 'Cosmodrama' and later on 'Dance of Life'.

The Cosmodrama programme lasts for a year and is organised in the form of four modules: *Consciousness and Reality; To Live or to Vegetate; The Obstacles to the Dance;* and *The Changing Relationship.* It is the result of a long effort to synthesise the different approaches and methods we have listed above.

The Art of Living in Peace programme is made up to some extent of a selection of the techniques most appropriate to achieving its aims.

The first part of this programme is specifically aimed at educators, while the second part is meant for everyone in general. However, it is absolutely necessary, for reasons we shall give at the beginning of the second part of the book, that future educators in this method should take part in the Art of Living in Peace training.

We shall now start by presenting the main theories that give rise to this new vision of education for peace.

The Non-Fragmentary Vision of Energy

The forms of manifestation of energy and corresponding sciences

Synoptic Table

Nature	Form of manifestation of energy	Matter	Life	Information
	Corresponding sciences	Physics	Biology	Computer science
Humans	Form of manifestation of energy	Body	Emotions	Mind
	Corresponding sciences	Anatomy	Physiology	Psychology
Society	Form of manifestation of energy	Housing and economy	Social life	Culture
	Corresponding sciences	Economics	Sociology	Anthropology

Figure 1

MODULE 2

THE PARADIGM SHIFT IN SCIENCE AND ITS INFLUENCE ON EDUCATION FOR PEACE

People interpret the words 'education' and 'peace' in several different ways according to their various points of view. These perspectives and differences in interpretation are mainly due to the extremely important influence of the Newtonian-Cartesian paradigm which has led human knowledge and our perception of the world into such a state of fragmentation and — as far as science is concerned — into such a degree of specialisation that we have lost contact with what is essential.

According to this perspective the world is a collection of solid elements related to each other by structures and systems ruled by mechanical laws. Such a vision has enabled humanity to make remarkable scientific discoveries and develop technological applications which have led to a level of material well-being previously unknown in our history.

But it is also true that this world view has generated a crisis of fragmentation that has reached the point of endangering the survival of all life-forms on the planet. We have arbitrarily cut up the world into territories which nations consider their sole property. We have divided knowledge into science, philosophy, art and religion.

Each of these fields has in turn been subdivided into count-less others, turning our universities into veritable 'towers of Babel'. We ourselves, as human beings, have been split into body, emotions, mind and intuition.

It is exactly such divisions that underlie all the different interpretations of what peace is, as well as of what hin-ders or brings peace about. This world view is also, of course, one of the main reasons why peace was lost in the first place. To show how peace is destroyed and how it can be rebuilt is precisely the aim of The Art of Living in Peace.

In addition, the fragmented world view has created different and often opposing perspectives and methods in the field of education.

We are witnesses to a transformation of our view of real-ity, to the birth of a new interdisciplinary and transdiscipli-nary paradigm which corresponds to a new vision of the world and of life. This new view, accompanied by a change in consciousness, is of a holistic nature. It is impor-tant that we are clearly aware of this transformation and of its considerable consequences for the subject of edu-cation for peace.

According to this point of view, which has arisen from the meeting of quantum physics with transpersonal psy-chology and the wisdom of the great spiritual traditions[1], the systems of the universe are all formed from the same energy[2], coming from a space which we know is not empty[3] but is made of a potential void which cannot be separated from the energy itself. From this point of view any kind of duality or fragmentation is seen as a product of the human mind whose essential quality is precisely to classify, divide and fragment, and then to establish rela-tionships between those tiny parts. Energy has three basic forms: matter, life and information. These forms are studied by the three main branches of science: physics, biology

and computer science which should be no more separated than the three human sciences, anatomy (body),
physiology (life) and psychology (consciousness), or the
three social sciences, anthropology (culture), sociology
(social and political life) and economics (production and
consumption).

We are now going to examine how the two perspectives and paradigms we have been discussing influence
ideas related to education and to peace. First of all, what
is peace?

A fragmentary vision of peace

A fragmentary vision of reality implies a separation
between subject and object. This perspective leads to a
fragmented view of peace. According to this view we can
identify two kinds of peace: external peace, or peace of
the 'object', and internal peace, or peace of the 'subject'. Let us consider these two aspects.

Peace as a phenomenon external to ourselves

From this point of view, peace is a cultural, judicial, political, social and socio-economic phenomenon. The result
is that peace is considered to belong to the area of the
social sciences, which indeed have made an effective
contribution to research into war and peace. The study of
conflicts was born from this perspective.[4]

We can also make two further distinctions: peace seen
as an absence of violence or war, and peace seen as a
state of harmony.

Peace seen as the absence of violence or war

This view indicates the need for some kind of treatment of
conflict and its causes, and general disarmament. In the

case of the former, peace would be the result of dealing with conflict, that is to say of the dissolution or transformation of the causes of the conflict. In the latter case, peace would be achieved by the elimination of the destructive aspects of conflict, i.e. violence and war; for some people conflict in itself presents some constructive dialectical aspects and evolutionary opportunities. Conflict is resolved through a *search for consensus*, which is one of the present concerns of Unesco.[5]

Lawyers would insist that the solution to conflict depends upon the transformation of the judicial concept of a 'fair war' into that of the right to peace or, in other words, the transformation of the *law of force into the force of the law*.[6] This concept validates the role of international courts in resolving conflicts based upon a fundamental legal principle: the right of human beings to live in peace.

We also have to work on preventing conflict. The Declaration of Human Rights addresses this need, complemented by the Declaration of Human Responsibilities.[7]

There is also a military assertion, which has existed since the dawn of time, that *if you want peace, you must prepare for war* — a principle that is taught and developed in military academies. It demonstrates a fundamental and important paradox: that the basis and role of armed forces is not to fight wars but to maintain peace by using force. This paradox reaches its culmination in the present form of the peace forces of the United Nations.

The opposing view would insist that *if you want peace, you should prepare for peace*. This perspective is responsible for efforts towards disarmament, begun during the era of the League of Nations, and those aimed at the demobilisation of armed forces. It is important to note that this latter idea can only be successfully put into practice if it is done on a totally multilateral basis — in other words, if it is undertaken by every nation without exception.

Otherwise we run the risk of seeing one nation that is still armed dominate the others which have disarmed. This is the main argument used by the heads of national armed forces to maintain and even develop their organisations.

Another perspective, the political one, shows how competition and nationalism constitute an important factor in war. The official solution to this is the establishment of a world government[7], for which the League of Nations and later the United Nations Organisation represent a preparatory phase.

Peace seen as a state of harmony and brotherhood between people and nations

According to this second approach, the state of peace would be the result of direct and constructive work done in groups and societies. It emphasises the education of societies by means of the mass media, with change on an intellectual level of public opinion and on a practical level of collective attitudes. This approach, which brings together education and the mass media, is also one of the main focuses of Unesco's work.[8]

The above two perspectives may be considered as belonging to a single category which we can call *social ecology*.

It is possible to extend the second perspective — peace as a state of harmony — to nature and the planet itself. This broader definition conforms to the recent recommendations of Unesco to include environmental problems with those of security and peace.[9] [10] A new conception of security has been born, as shown by the Brundtland Report.[11] Thus, peace is linked to the ecology of the planet.

Now let us move on to look at the idea of peace of the

'subject' or inner peace.

Peace as an inner state of consciousness

Since wars begin 'in the minds of men', as stated in Unesco's constitution, it is up to Unesco and the schools all over the world to put an end to the beginning of war.

Robert Muller. Speech made as co-winner of Unesco's Peace Education Award. Unesco, September 20, 1989.

The idea of peace as an inner state of being corresponds to the contents of the preamble to Unesco's Constitution which states that 'since wars begin in the minds of men, it is in the minds of men that the defences of peace must be constructed'.[12] This concept could be called *inner or personal ecology.*

Although often quoted, this preamble is rarely put into practice in real life, as shown by a short study which we recently published.[13] This study is based on information provided by Unesco (Berg, 1988[14]) and underlines the following facts: Among 310 institutions dedicated to education and research on peace, only 24 (5%) of the subjects taught related to inner peace, while maybe up to 14% of research was focused on this area.

One of the prophecies in the Bible states that swords will be beaten into ploughshares. It is possible to interpret this statement symbolically: it is within each human being that aggression and violence, represented by the sword, must be transformed into an energy of peace, represented by the ploughshare.

Some more or less successful efforts towards general disarmament on an exterior level may lead us to believe that this is all that is needed to establish peace. We have already mentioned this idea, when we were discussing peace viewed simply as an absence of conflict. Let us look at it again in connection with this prophecy: even if we destroy all our weapons, right down to the last gun — in other words, if we get rid of all the swords — unless we transform our inner selves, we shall still fight one another with our ploughshares . . . .

This explains why the Yamoussoukro Declaration on Peace in the Minds of Men was written.[15]

As before, we are again faced with two theories.

Peace as a result of the absence or dissolution of inner psychic conflicts is a psychotherapeutic concept. It is in eliminating the conflict between the ego and superego, between the heart and the mind, or between the intuition and the heart, for example, that it is possible to re-establish inner peace.

Peace as a state of inner harmony is a result of inner work which involves a non-fragmented vision of reality on the intellectual level, a detachment from any sort of concept, being or object. It comes from the birth of a 'natural' wisdom, which is bound up with altruistic love. It is a *spiritual concept*, linked to the great spiritual traditions of humanity,[16] and also to recent research in transpersonal psychology. We would like to point out in passing that we see here one of the results of the fragmentation of knowledge that characterises the established paradigm, in that psychology has become separated from the spiritual traditions.

In conclusion, we can say that the fragmented vision of peace leads us to reductionist ideas which in themselves are an expression of the over-specialisation and fragmentation of knowledge. Thus we are faced with various incompatible definitions.

A holistic vision of peace

A new vision of peace will be a holistic one or, in other words, a non-fragmented vision. It will come about as a result of an approach which takes into account all the different points of view. It implies:

- A non-fragmentary theory of space-energy in which energy manifests in the form of matter, life and information.

- A perspective which takes into account human beings, society and the natural world or, in other words, inner or personal ecology, social ecology and planetary ecology. These three aspects are intimately linked and constantly interacting. From this perspective peace is concurrently an inner state of consciousness arising from personal tranquillity, a state of social accord dependent upon an ability to solve conflicts peacefully, and a state of harmony with nature.

So we cannot have true peace on a personal level if we know that poverty and violence hold sway on the social level or that the natural world threatens to destroy us because we are destroying it.

The holistic vision or consciousness implies a progressive broadening of consciousness. It begins with a personal awareness and dissolution of egocentric aspects and a progression towards a social consciousness, although still an anthropocentric one — in other words seen from an exclusively human viewpoint. As and when society realises the extent of its dependence on the planet and all its life forms, social consciousness will evolve into planetary consciousness. Even then this will still be to some extent geocentric, with its perspective somewhat limited to our planet, regarding it as the centre of the universe. The holistic vision, therefore, is a cosmic consciousness of a transpersonal, transsocial and transplanetary nature, which integrates these three aspects into a broader perspective.

The study and administration of peace must be the result of interdisciplinary and transdisciplinary work.

Just as peace can be viewed from a fragmentary perspective or a holistic one, so has education too been fragmented and distorted. It is obvious that the time has come for a new approach. It is this that we are going to look at now, beginning with a summary of the effects of the established paradigm on education.

The fragmented view of education

What is called education today is very often confused with teaching. Teaching is aimed only at a person's intellectual or sensory capabilities. It is no more than a mental communication which adds to our amount of knowledge or influences our opinions.

This kind of teaching has become the exclusive domain of schools, while it is assumed that the family takes responsibility for character development, which includes feelings, emotions, habits and inner attitudes.

In fact, everything indicates that families are increasingly copying schools; the excessive breadth of curriculum is to a large extent disrupting the relationship between parents and children. The family is progressively becoming an extension of school.

This has led to a schism between thought and action, between on the one hand opinions and attitudes fostered to a large extent by school, and on the other hand the habits and behaviour instilled by the family.

We would like to mention at this point the results of surveys of racial attitudes in certain countries. If we consult public opinion, a large majority of whites say they oppose racism. This is almost certainly something they learned at school. But if they are asked whether they would allow their daughter to marry a black man, the response of that same majority is negative. This answer must arise from the traditions and habits of the family. Other examples

<u>Visions of Peace</u>

according to the old and new paradigms

Synoptic Table

Established paradigm	Holistic paradigm
Peace seen as an external phenomenon	*Peace seen as an external and internal phenomenon*
On the *external level* peace is seen:	Peace is the result of a convergence of measures relating to *inner ecology, social ecology* and *planetary ecology*, in which the principal theories of the established paradigm are taken into consideration and find their place in an integrated manner.
1. *As the absence of conflict and violence.* Many theories: cultural, judicial, socio-economic, military, religious.	
2. *As a state of harmony and brotherhood* between people and with nature.	This convergence results in a transpersonal state of consciousness, of which peace is one of the manifestations.
3. On the *inner level* peace is seen as the absence or result of dissolution of intra-psychological conflicts, known as a *state of inner harmony.*	
There is a lack of integration of these various points of view.	

Figure 2

abound: it is possible to have democratic opinions and behave tyrannically, to defend the environment and step on flowers and ants, to declare yourself non-violent and hit your children, to claim to be tolerant and gossip behind everybody's back.

Confusing teaching with education brings about another fragmentation to the extent that knowledge is continuously broken down into further specialities and sub-specialities, as is the case in secondary teaching and even more so in higher education.

The holistic approach in education offers us an entirely different array of techniques, which we will now discuss.

The holistic view of education

When education is confused with teaching, the accent is placed on the mind. A holistic approach aims to awaken and develop the intuition as much as the mind and the feelings as much as the senses. The goal is to achieve a balance between these psychic functions. As far as the brain is concerned, this would correspond to a balance between its right and left hemispheres and to circulation of energy between the cortical and sub-cortical layers, as well as throughout the whole cerebro-spinal system.

Whereas teaching emphasises the contents of a course and the acquisition of facts, the holistic approach shows us how every situation in life offers us the opportunity to learn; moreover there is an emphasis on developing the ability to teach ourselves. The global and specific contexts of every situation take on an equal importance.

Traditional education has a tendency to condition people to live exclusively in the outer world, while the holistic approach orients them towards the inner world as well as the outer. We could also make a comparison between the orientation of the contents of traditional education

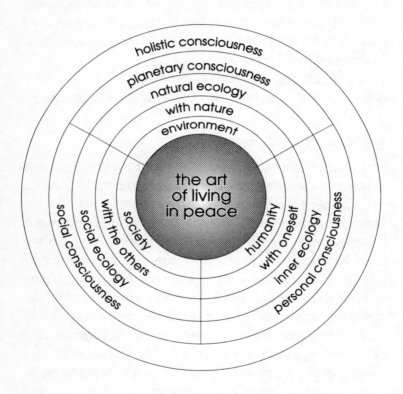

Figure 3

and those of holistic education. The first approach emphasises consumption, aggressive competition, success, excessive specialisation, acquisition and material affluence. The holistic approach demands voluntary simplicity, cooperation, human values, general knowledge prior to specialised knowledge, and sees money as something to be used to serve fundamental values rather than as an end in itself.

In addition to all these differences, there is a basic one which lies in the concept of human evolution and our capacity for transformation.

The established paradigm is in the grip of a static perspective in the sense that there is a general belief that our intellectual and emotional development ceases after adolescence. From the holistic point of view, evolution continues after adolescence. In fact it acknowledges that we can go through a complete metamorphosis, like that of caterpillar to butterfly. Metaphorically speaking, the caterpillar symbolises the human being tied into a web of habits, prejudices and daily routines. The chrysalis represents the process of transformation from a consciousness of egoism, withdrawal, limitation and fear, to one of breadth, harmony and altruism. It involves a period of inner crisis, a questioning of previous values, a temporary dark night of the soul. The butterfly would be the new state of consciousness characterised by a state of peace and fulfilment.

A few words here about educational methodology. According to the traditional mechanistic paradigm the student is seen as a piece of magnetic tape or a blank film onto which the teacher mechanically transfers the lesson. The student is expected to make an effort to memorise things in order to reinforce the teacher's work. The process is expected to bring about the changes recommended in the lesson. Instead of being the object of teaching, the new paradigm replaces the concept of

The Old and New Paradigms in Education
Synoptic Table

	Established paradigm	Holistic paradigm
Concept of education	Information. Teaching limited to the intellect. Instruction aimed at memory and reason.	Training. Education of the whole person. Process of harmonisation and full development of senses, feelings, reason and intuition.
Concept of student	The pupil considered as an 'object', as an automatic mechanism of recording.	The pupil considered as a 'subject', as an active participant in the educative process.
Nervous system	Left side of brain.	Left and right sides of brain. The whole cerebro-spinal system.
Field of action	Acquisition of knowledge; accent on content. Changing of opinions.	Transformation of the personality in its entirety. Changing of opinions, attitudes and behaviours.
Educative agent	School as an agent of intellectual education, with the family as an auxiliary of school. The educator as 'teacher'.	Family, school and society in a joint effort. The educator as animator, facilitator, focaliser and even catalyst for evolution.
Concept of evolution	Evolution ceases at adolescence. Maturity limited to the intellect, to the capacity to procreate and to work. This evolution is personal.	Evolution continues with adulthood. Maturity seen as a state of broadened consciousness, of harmony, fulfilment and peace of a personal and transpersonal nature.
Type of training. Orientation of values.	Predominance of specialisation. Pragmatic values: consumption, competition, power, possessiveness, celebrity.	General training takes precedence over specialisation. Pragmatic and ethical values: voluntary simplicity, cooperation, generosity, sharing, equality, equanimity.
Methods of education	Verbal explanation, spoken, complemented by books and textbooks. *Passive method.* Rewards and punishments in a selective and competitive system. The teacher teaches, the pupil listens. School separate from the community. The teacher 'recommends' opinions, attitudes and changes of behaviour.	Research and individual and group study. Spoken verbal presentations by students and teacher. *Active method.* Audiovisual methods. Presentations, excursions, visits. Student is active, does research and teaches others. The teacher as advisor, consultant, guide. School integrated into the community. Educator is a living example of the principles and behaviour he recommends.

Figure 4

passive students with that of students who actively participate in the process, who take their transformation into their own hands and chart their own course.

It is in this direction that since the beginning of the century we have been witnessing a very slow evolution in educational methods. 'Active' education is gradually replacing 'passive' education. The slowness of its adoption is due to centuries of deeply rooted habits which delay the assumption of new attitudes.

In this new or active kind of education it is up to the student to work, to undertake research, to visit places, to make observations on the ground, to create personal written or oral reports. In this latter case it is the student who gives the lesson; the teacher becomes the expert, the consultant; he gives pointers rather than teaches. He provides an example by his behaviour, showing that the principles he advocates are deeply rooted in his daily life.

The scope of this work does not allow us to expand on the subject of active education. There are numerous studies on this topic and various methods of applying it, and it has proved to be more effective in encouraging the evolution of the person as a whole than have traditional teaching techniques.

Before concluding this section I would like to draw your attention to the fact that both the shift in paradigm and the change in educational methods are a specific phenomenon of the industrialised societies as well as those that have been influenced by the western world. It seems that societies that live in harmony with nature and are more closely integrated into their environment use methods of education which are rooted in action and which count on the participation of the whole community.

Now that we have defined peace and education in relation to the paradigm shift, we can go on to discuss the nature of education for peace.

Towards a holistic view of education for peace

As we have seer., the traditional Newtonian-Cartesian paradigm has brought us — both despite and partly as a consequence of the enormous benefits and luxuries it provides — to the verge of destroying the planet and to violent solutions to conflicts.

This paradigm also provides us with a muddled and fragmented vision of peace and a reductionist view of education, with confusion between real education and mere intellectual instruction.

According to the holistic paradigm, education for peace is based on a new vision of education and a new sense of peace, as described above. We could define holistic education for peace as follows:

Holistic education for peace is a method of education inspired by active methods, directed to the person as a whole to help him or her maintain or re-establish harmony between senses, feelings, mind and intuition. It is concerned with physical health, along with emotional and mental equilibrium, and the awakening and sustenance of human values.

Everything which exists is part of an interdependent universe. All living beings depend on one another for their existence, well-being and development.

Declaration of Human Responsibilities for Peace and Sustainable Development. Article 1, University of Peace, Costa Rica, 1989.

On the social level, holistic education for peace addresses the task of developing the skills with which to manage conflicts in a non-violent manner and to transform destructive forms of energy into constructive action on the cultural, social, political and economic levels.

As far as the relationship between humans and the environment is concerned, the aim of holistic education is to teach people to repair, to whatever extent possible, the ecological destruction caused by humans and to maintain the balance of the ecosystem.

Basically, then, it is about instilling an 'art of living in peace'. This art must be developed on three levels:

- *Human:* inner ecology or the art of living in peace with oneself
- *Social:* social ecology or the art of living in peace with others
- *Environmental:* planetary ecology or the art of living in peace with nature

On the human level this education will awaken simultaneously or in succession:

- Peace of the body
- Peace of the heart[18]
- Peace of the mind

On the social level the art of living in peace is addressed to three different areas:

- The economy
- Social and political life
- Culture

On the environmental level holistic education will look for the best solutions for living in peace with the environment, while taking into consideration the three different forms of energy:

- Matter (solid, liquid, fire, gas)
- Life (vegetable, animal and human)

● Information (atomic, genetic, cerebral)

Doing this will broaden the field of consciousness in three areas:

● Personal egocentric consciousness
● Social anthropocentric consciousness
● Planetary geocentric consciousness

In going beyond these three forms of awareness, the art of living in peace opens doors to the holistic vision characterised by a transpersonal state of cosmic consciousness.

This, then, is a general outline of holistic education for peace as taught by The Art of Living in Peace. Before concluding this section, a few words about a basic methodological principle: Holistic education for peace cannot be limited to the classroom; it is an apprenticeship in which self-training must be encouraged.

The work we present in this book is an attempt to develop a self-training programme, in the sense discussed by Abraham Moles in a recent Unesco publication,[19] where he introduces the concept of self-learning. It is an invitation, even though part of a course, to explore and verify through personal experience the foundations of thousands of years of traditional wisdom, checked and verified to some degree by modern science, in the spirit of Unesco's Venice Declaration.

What we are proposing here is a system in which, to quote Abraham Moles, education would tend 'once again to merge with the uncertainties of daily life; it would regain some of the characteristics of direct apprenticeship which the tribe or old-style village offered to its young people outside school.'[20]

REFERENCES

NB Where English-language editions of the publications which appear in the reference lists have not been traced or do not exist, the French editions cited in the original work are listed.

1. This meeting of disciplines is the objective of the recommendations of the Declaration of Venice, issued under the aegis of Unesco. See *Science and the Boundaries of Knowledge*. Paris, Unesco, 1987.

2. Lupasco, S. *Les Trois Matières*. Paris, Julliard, 1960.

3. Norel, G. *Histoire de la Matière et de la Vie. Les transformations de l'énergie et de l'évolution*. Paris, Maloine, Collection Recherches Interdisciplinaires, 1984.

4. Bosc, R.*Sociologie de la Paix*. Paris, Spes, 1965.

5. M'Bow Amadou-Mahtar et al. *Consensus and Peace*. Paris, Unesco, 1980.

6. Ferencz, B.B. & Keyes, Ken. *Planethood: The Key to Your Future*. Preface by Robert Muller. Love Line Books (US), 1991.

7. A world constitutive assembly, held in Innsbruck, Austria, adopted a constitution for the federation of the planet. A congress was organised in Tours in 1990.

8. Unesco. *Media Education*. Paris, Unesco, 1985.

9. Unesco. *Recommendations Concerning Education for International Understanding, Cooperation and Peace and Education Relating to Human Rights and Fundamental Freedoms*. Paris, Unesco, 1974

10. Unesco. *Yamoussoukro Declaration on Peace in the Minds of Men*. Paris, Unesco, 1989.

11. Brundtland, G.H. et al. *Our Common Future*. Oxford/New York, OUP, 1987. Part III, Ch. 11.

12. *Unesco Constitution*. Paris, Unesco.

13. *Peace in the Spirit of Man. A forgotten basic principle of Unesco*. IPRA, Congrès International, 1988.

14. Unesco & Berg. *World Directory of Peace Research and Training Institutions.* Paris, Unesco, 1992.

15. See no. 10.

16. Krishnamurti. *The First and Last Freedom.* Foreword by Aldous Huxley. HarperCollins.

17. Weil, Pierre. *L'Homme Sans Frontières.* Paris, L'Espace Bleu, 1989.

18. A recent Unesco study recommends a 'socioaffective' approach, based on experience. See *Education for International Cooperation and Peace at the Primary School Level.* Paris, Unesco, 1985.

19. Moles, A. In *Media Education.* Paris, Unesco, 1985.

20. Ibid.

Methods of Education

In the short, medium and long terms the reading of this general introduction can be enriched by the following activities:

- Discussion groups on the various themes
- Visiting educational institutions which practise these active methods of education
- Group study and discussion of the paradigm shift

We recommend the following authors:

- Capra, F. *The Turning Point.* Bantam/Flamingo, 1983.
- Kuhn, T. *The Structure of Scientific Revolutions.* University of Chicago Press, 1970.
- Ferguson, M. *The Aquarian Conspiracy.* Tarcher (US) / Paladin (UK), 1982.
- Bohm, D. *The Undivided Universe.* London, Routledge.
- Weil, P. *L'Homme Sans Frontières.* Paris, L'Espace Bleu, 1989.
- Weil, P. *Vers un Approche Holistique de la Nature de la Realité.* In Question No. 64, Paris, Albin Michel, 1986.
- Nicolescu, B. *Nous, la Particle et le Monde.* Paris, Le Mail, 1985.

MODULE 3

TRAINING OTHERS IN THE ART OF LIVING IN PEACE

Prerequisites for a peace educator

For peace educators to be able to pass on the Art of Living in Peace to other people, whether children, teenagers or adults, they must fulfil an essential preliminary condition: they themselves must be an example of what they teach. One could say that their very being, by radiating qualities such as affection, gentleness, patience, openness to the needs of others, the ability to put themselves in somebody else's shoes, and so on, would render all other forms of instruction unnecessary.

The essential question, then, is to know how to find such educators or, if they are few and far between, which seems to be the case, how to train and prepare them.

In the first case, it is a matter of choice — of recruitment and selection. In the second case, it is a matter of training.

In fact the qualities necessary in a peace educator are very similar to those of outstanding individuals, the great Masters, examples of whom exist in all cultures — men and women who have integrated wisdom and love into their everyday existence and who have dedicated their lives to the service of these values.

These people, even though they exist in our day, are rare. A Gandhi or a Mother Teresa isn't born every day.

What we can do is to find people who identify with the masters or with these qualities, who work on themselves and who have sufficient clarity and modesty to show themselves as they really are, while in the first place behaving in harmony with the great human values such as truth, beauty and altruistic love. Some such people exist and fortunately all indications are that they are gradually growing in number as the threat of extinction of life on the planet increases.

To give these people an additional training which will allow them to pass on the Art of Living in Peace, while concurrently training themselves with the methods outlined in this book, is the sensible solution which we have devised.

To this end, it is necessary that future educators in the Art of Living in Peace undergo the same learning process, for the reasons stated above.

We shall begin with a description of the process of the destruction of peace.

The destruction of peace

In order to know how to awaken and rebuild peace, nothing is more necessary than an in-depth understanding of the process that has led the human race to risk destroying life on the planet, without even taking into account the slaughter of the last two world wars.

We are going to present a basic theory of this process using short statements, each of which is a summary of theoretical points of view or of results of research in the different areas of science or traditional wisdom.

Each statement can be developed according to the interests of students and the amount of time available for covering the whole programme. The set of statements can be presented on computer disk, projected on a screen or written on a blackboard, for purposes of group

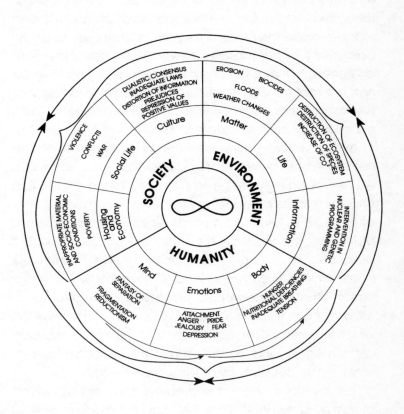

Figure 5

discussion. (See Figure 5)

The art of living in peace with oneself

How was war born in the human mind?

As the preamble to Unesco's Constitution says so well, it is effectively in our mind — in other words, at the level of our thoughts and emotions — that the seeds of violence and war are born. They later take root in our physical body, particularly in our muscles. Nevertheless, this statement isn't enough. It runs the risk of becoming dogma if we do not attempt to demonstrate the process in an experimental or experiential fashion. Simply examining our own experience confirms this preamble.

In fact we have already given above a general outline of the phenomenon of the seeding of violence, when we described how the general process of the destruction of peace takes place. To understand this process better at the human level, we must go deeper and describe in detail how this destruction happens within ourselves. This description will be accompanied by real-life experiences in line with the recommendations which follow this explanation. These experiences provide an opportunity to escape from the intellectual and explanatory level on which we are meeting now, in reading the intellectual part of this module, and to confirm in real life — in the flesh, literally — the authenticity of these statements.

It is a vicious circle of compulsive repetition, in which almost all of humanity finds itself caught, a kind of optical illusion.

This process takes place almost simultaneously on three basic levels which correspond, as we have already seen, to the three basic forms of energy:

● The mental level and our thoughts and concepts

Fundamental Theory of
the Process of the Destruction of Peace

Unesco's Declaration of Venice recommends the reconciliation of the sciences and the spiritual traditions.

This coming together leads to an ultimate conception of reality: an infinite and atemporal primordial space.

From this space emanates the energy of all the known systems.

This energy takes three indivisible forms:
● Informational (intelligence)
● Biological (life)
● Physical (matter)

This, then, is a non-fragmentary theory of energy.

Human beings are an integral part of this energy system.

They also are made of:
● Matter (body)
● Life (emotions)
● Information (mind)
inseparable from the whole

But by means of thought human beings separate themselves from the universe. They create a fantasy of separation:
● Humans — the universe
● Me — the world
● Subject — object

The human mind creates boundaries in space. But space does not have any limits.

Figure 6a (continued overleaf)

By their thoughts human beings separate themselves from society and from nature. In their mind they forget that Nature, Society and Humankind are inseparable. Moreover, mind is separated from the information of the whole. Human mind is separated from the universal mind. Within the individual, mind separates itself from the emotions (life) and from the body (matter).

So a process of destruction of the personal ecology begins. A fragmentation affects the human being. In his mind the fantasy of separation engenders a paradigm of separation.

Because he feels fragmented, he generates destructive emotions on the level of life, specifically attachment and possessiveness of people, things and ideas which give him pleasure. These destructive emotions generate stress, which destroys the equilibrium of the body.

Because people believe they are separate from society, they create a piecemeal culture, a violent social life and exploitative economic conditions.

The individual projects his or her fragmentation on the level of knowledge.

These social conditions reinforce in their turn the suffering of the individual.

A society which exploits human beings increases separation and grows into an unbridled exploitation of nature. It intervenes in information, in the nuclear industry and genetic manipulation. It destroys the ecosystems and threatens life on the planet. Lastly, it destroys and pollutes the elements of matter.

And this is how the self-reinforcing vicious circle of self-destruction of humankind and of planetary life functions

The function of holistic education for peace is to transform these obstacles into positive forms of energy (see Figure 6b).

Fiigure 6a continued

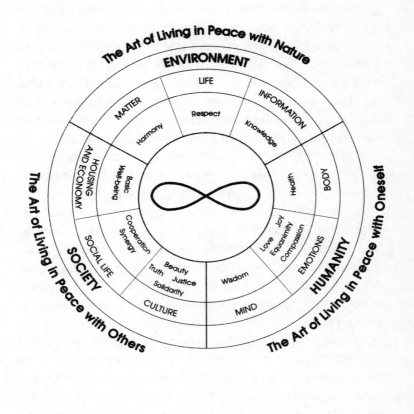

Fiigure 6b

● The emotional level of our life
● The level of our physical body

It would be helpful to study Figure 6 along with this explanation.

On the mental level an illusion takes shape which we call the *fantasy of separation*. It is a permanent phenomenon of our mental world. It consists of the belief that we are separate from the outside world, that the 'I' and the universe do not have any connection with each other.

It is possible to create an experience of this in a very simple way. Point with your finger to where nature is and where the universe is. Our immediate reaction is to point our finger outside ourselves, at trees, at the garden or at anything outside our own bodies. It is at that moment that the separation of subject and object takes place.

This separation has a long history and starts very early. Some people believe it begins when the baby sees his mother's breast, or at birth, or even before that.

In fact, this separation is only an appearance; it has the practical function of bringing us into existence but in reality it is illusory. If, for example, we examine under an electron microscope the human body, the air or any object, we cannot avoid concluding, as is shown by quantum physics, that there is nothing there except space-energy. At the final count, when someone looks at something, it is as if space is looking at space across space. All indications are that this space is a void which is not empty. It is full of the potential of everything that exists. From the moment when we begin to regard the outside world as separate, we start to create limits in our minds, imaginary frontiers. All conflicts are born on these frontiers. In fact space does not have any frontiers — it is all one, a continuum.

Another direct consequence of this fantasy of separation is that the subject, believing in his own solidity and that of the external world, becomes attached to everything that is pleasurable, rejects everything that is likely to cause him displeasure or suffering, and remains indifferent to all else.

In fact, everything indicates that we are made for pleasure, joy and happiness. We spend our lives in search of these things. Except we only look for them outside ourselves. We could call it *the neurosis of paradise lost*. The lost paradise exists within ourselves. Peace is part of this lost paradise. It is a mood or state of consciousness. The problem is not pleasure in itself, but our attachment to the object which gives us pleasure.

After the establishment of the fantasy of separation we became attached to objects, people or ideas.

The emotional reaction that generally follows the attachment is fear: fear of losing or being robbed of the object which we think we possess. Whether it is a jewel, a lover or a good idea, the pattern is the same.

Fear of loss gives rise to destructive emotions like distrust, jealousy, aggression, wounded pride and depression.

These emotions are responsible for and constitute stress; they form a whole which can be called mental suffering. But stress also causes us to experience physical pain through sickness.

Mental suffering and physical pain in their turn strengthen and reinforce the fantasy of separation.

This is how the personal vicious circle of compulsive repetition is formed, which leads to the loss of our inner, interpersonal and social peace.

METHODS OF EDUCATION

Phase 1

As we have mentioned before, during this phase it is important that the student, or better still the 'trainee', observes by himself and within himself the truth of these statements. He has to discover to what extent he is a victim of the vicious circle of compulsive repetition and to what extent he is controlled by the neurosis of paradise lost.

Short-term

1. Start with a theoretical explanation, accompanied by a diagram (Figure 7).

2. In order to demonstrate the fantasy of separation, ask your students to point to nature.

3. Invite the group to role-play on the following theme:

● A young man and woman meet for the first time; it is love at first sight; they set up a date in a café; this meeting is interrupted by the young man's lover; a scene of anger and jealousy; the young woman falls ill; her mother calls the doctor.

● Group discussion with the help of Figure 7.

Medium- and long-term

1. Use the above short-term programme as an introduction, then continue with a long course and study of the fundamental theory of the destruction of peace; historical research on the process of fragmentation and destruction of peace.

2. Make a wall newspaper, where the 'trainees' periodically stick cuttings from magazines and newspapers

illustrating the consequences of attachment and possessiveness in individual and collective life.

3. Organise a series of discussions where students use personal case histories illustrating the vicious circle of compulsive repetition.

4. Invite an expert in group dynamics or encounter groups to help the group discover its own inner obstacles to peace.

5. Analyse a historical conflict which took place in your country, applying the contents of Figure 7.

Phase 2

Short-term. The first phase provokes a strong motivation in a large number of trainees to discover a means of breaking out of the vicious circle. The group is then ready to embark on the rest of the programme: the awakening and development of inner peace.

The awakening and development of inner peace

To achieve this, it is best to begin with the body. As we have seen, it is possible to distinguish various seats of inner peace: *peace of the body, peace of the heart* and *peace of mind.*

This phase exists mainly to allow trainees to locate within themselves and get in touch with the different kinds of inner peace. These are so interdependent that it is difficult to distinguish between them; if we do so, it is only as an aid to understanding them; otherwise it would mean reverting to the kind of fragmentation which we are trying to leave behind.

Therefore peace of the body also involves the other two aspects of inner peace.

Peace of the body

Our body is a physical system of dense energy, of matter through which vital and psychic energy circulates. This energy is given different names depending on the cultural milieu. In yoga it is called *prana*, in Tibet *rlung*, in Greece *pneuma*, in Hebrew *ruach*; in China it is known as *ki*, in Polynesia as *mana*, among the Dakota as *wakanda*, and in ancient Egypt it was called *ka*.

According to these traditions, this energy circulates through subtle channels which are well known in Chinese acupuncture and in Chinese and Japanese micromassage. Free circulation of this energy and its balanced distribution throughout the body would correspond to a state of harmony and peace. Destructive emotions, as described above, create among other effects blockages in the form of more or less chronic knots of muscular tension depending on the occurrence of emotional crises during the course of life.

We find similar concepts in psychotherapy and psychology. Different schools give energy different names: *libido* (Freud, Jung), *orgone* (Reich), *élan vital* (Bergson), psychotronic energy (Krippner). Unblocking these knots of tension, relaxing what Reich called character armour, is what both traditional methods and modern bioenergetic methods are trying to achieve. From the moment one is able to undo these knots of tension, one's energy once again becomes available and starts to circulate again throughout one's whole body.

The main effect of this is a state of peace, of tranquillity, which fosters a broader state of consciousness and a harmonious psychosomatic condition.

Some of the methods, among others, for achieving this are: relaxation as practised in yoga, particularly hatha yoga; T'ai Chi Chuan, which is like a slow dance; and the non-violent martial arts like Japanese judo and aikido.

Yoga relaxation has inspired research in the field of psychosomatic medicine. Due particularly to the 'autogenic training' of Schultz[1] and Caycedo's sophrology[2], there is no longer any doubt that this approach provides a physical base for peace of the emotions and the mind. Psychophysical measurements have amply confirmed what we all experience in our own lives.

A programme aimed at personal experience and at achieving this first kind of peace, has to begin with some form of relaxation. Relaxation provides the following advantages:

- It enables us to create a somatic basis for inner peace.
- It allows us to go through the day in a calm state, if it is practised every morning.
- It helps to keep us healthy.
- It aids medical treatment in the healing of a large number of psychosomatic illnesses.
- It helps to alleviate or even quickly eliminate a nervous or tense state.
- It cures insomnia.
- It does away with sleepiness during the day.
- It facilitates creativity.
- It leads us into other states of consciousness.
- It is a preparation for meditation (see later).

A healthy and balanced diet reinforces the peace of the body. Yoga, for example, teaches us that there are three kinds of food: heavy foods which encourage torpor and passivity, energising foods which stir us up and push us to physical activity, and those foods which facilitate harmony and inner peace. Yoga recommends a natural and vegetarian diet. It is interesting to note that a reduction in human consumption of meat would free up agricultural land for sufficient food production to eliminate hunger in the developing countries.[3]

Peace of the heart

As we have stated previously, the emotional and affec-
tive aspects of peace are too often neglected in research
and education for peace, due to a predominantly intellectual approach. Yet it is evident to all who are concerned with feelings and emotions that they play as fundamental a role in inner and even social peace as they
do in violence and war. What is inner peace if not a state
of harmony and fulfilment, where feelings of joy and love
can find free expression?

What can we pass on to our `trainees' in peace? How
to create peace on a feeling level? This is a very important question.

Various answers have been given to this question. Each
one recommends a method for attaining peace. Some
are very simple and can be practised by anyone. Others
require the guidance of a Master or a therapist, depending on the culture in which we live.

We shall attempt to give here a very short description
of these methods. A great deal of study and comparative research on the results obtained is necessary in the
field of experimental education in order to determine
which techniques are the most effective. But there is to
some extent a consensus that the ability of the educator
to give of himself with devotion and love is as important,
or even more so, than the actual method itself. One can
also imagine that the motivation and devotion of the
`trainee' is essential for the ongoing practice of each
technique.

It is possible to distinguish two major categories of methods: those which take as their point of departure the
destructive emotions like hate and anger, and those
which tend to awaken and develop the positive emotions
which lead to peace. These latter are inseparable from

peace of the mind and even that of the body, and we deal with them later on.

Methods of energy transformation

We shall now discuss the methods which deal with destructive emotions with a view to transforming or dissolving them — without, however, suppressing them.

● *Direct awareness*

This is the simplest method. It consists of recognising the destructive emotion at the moment when it appears. According to the yoga tradition, and in particular the Tibetan one, there are five factors or 'poisons' that destroy peace, of which four are of a purely emotional nature and the fifth is cognitive. This last one refers to the fantasy of separation and is called ignorance or misconception.

The other four, which are related to one another, are attachment, anger, jealousy and pride. It is at the moment when these emotions come into being that we can become aware of them. To start with, this direct awareness of the emotion's origin comes too late — for example, anger may have already produced its effects. All we can do at this stage is to recognise that we have been taken over by the emotion. Gradually we become aware when it is happening and eventually we are able to see it coming. This last is the ideal condition. Experience suggests that when we are able to do this, our anger dissolves and its energy transforms into positive feelings.

● *Gandhi's 'ahimsa' method of non-violence*

Advocated by Gandhi, ahimsa means far more than non-violence. It is about transforming feelings of hate into feelings of love. The success of Gandhi in bringing about the independence of India through nation-wide non-

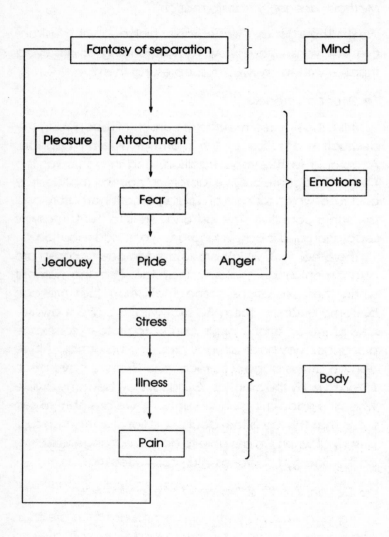

Figure 7

violent action constitutes a very impressive demonstration of the power of ahimsa. Used in a number of countries today, it requires total self-awareness and constant attention to what is going on within oneself.[4]

● *Psychotherapeutic methods*

For many people the above methods fail because of deeply-rooted negative habits and ingrained parental and cultural models, and more particularly because of identification with educators who are themselves violent. Often a child's violent reactions cannot be expressed and they remain blocked in the body and the mind until adulthood; they still want to be expressed and they eventually burst out in an inadequate and compulsive manner.

In this book we shall confine ourselves to talking about only some of the therapeutic techniques which aim at unblocking and freeing violence and the seeds of aggression. Today hundreds of psychotherapeutic methods exist, among which are: Freudian psychoanalysis, Jungian analysis, Moreno's psychodrama, Fritz Perls's gestalt therapy, Wilhelm Reich's orgone therapy, Lowen's bioenergetics, Desoille's daydream therapy, Assagioli's psychosynthesis, Carl Rogers's person-centred therapy and Victor Frankl's logotherapy.

The peace educator cannot absorb all these techniques, nor can she apply them, for that is something that requires a long training. She can, however, undertake one of them, which seems to fulfil her own personal needs. This will help her to recognise the needs of her own 'trainees' and to guide them, as necessary, towards a particular therapy or therapist.

Instead of trying to transform a heart of conflict into a heart of peace, it is possible to awaken peace directly.

Responsibility is an inherent aspect of any relation in which human beings are involved. This capacity to act responsibly in a conscious, independent, unique and personal manner is an inalienable creative quality of every human being. There is no limit to its scope or depth other than that established by each person for himself. The more it is acted upon and put into practice, the more it will grow and become strengthened.

Declaration of Human Responsibilities for Lasting Peace and Sustainable Development. Article 6, Chapter III. University of Peace, Costa Rica, 1989.

Direct methods of awakening peace

In each one of us slumber the functions or qualities of heart that are directly responsible for maintaining inner and social peace. The spiritual traditions are unanimous on this point. We can summarise these qualities as follows:

- *Joy.* We are made, as we have already mentioned, for a life of joy, especially the kind we experience when we see the joy of others.
- *Altruistic love.* This can be defined as a feeling of wanting everybody's happiness and acting accordingly.
- *Compassion.* How can we live in peace knowing that suffering and poverty exist all around us? Compassion is precisely the feeling of wanting to heal these ills and of moving heaven and earth to achieve it.
- *The universality* of the above three feelings is very important; they apply to every living species without bias. If they were really put into practice by everybody towards everybody else, would there still be wars and conflicts?

These qualities can be awakened and developed in different ways.

In the first place this can be achieved by the *example* of the educator who interiorises them and integrates them into his daily life. One cannot emphasise this point enough.

We can also call on *methods of visualisation* such as are employed in daydream therapy and, more specifically, in psychosynthesis. This involves asking students, when they are in a relaxed state, to imagine from time to time an actual scene from their daily lives where these qualities are put into practice. It is a mind-programming which facilitates the following method.

This consists of *informing the student about these qualities* by defining them, as we have done here, and encouraging their application in daily life, showing the student that this path leads to peace.

Since the methods for awakening peace of the heart are inseparable from those for awakening peace of mind, we shall now proceed to concentrate on these.

Peace of mind

First let us turn our attention to the term 'mind'. On the one hand it can refer to the collection of mental faculties we possess, such as intelligence, perception, memory and so on. On the other hand it also refers to a form of subtle energy, called 'spiritual energy' by Bergson, to a principle of life, consciousness and thought, as opposed to the body which is made of matter. In this sense it is linked to moral or so-called 'higher' values.

The holistic view goes beyond any kind of opposites or dualities, embracing and integrating them. Thanks to the non-fragmentary theory of energy, in which the lines of expression assume three forms of an opposing and independent appearance — matter (body), life (movement and emotions) and information (psyche) — but are in fact linked in a continuous evolutionary chain, the duality of matter and mind tends to dissolve.

That is why we are adopting a wider approach of spirituality and the mind. This term indicates a stage at which everything is beyond the mind and the psyche and which integrates and comprises them.[5] In this sense the human being would be an energy transformer, the same energy, whether manifested as matter, life or mind. What we call mind is nothing other, perhaps, than energy itself in its primordial state and which through human beings returns to that state.

Everything indicates that total peace is achieved in this transpersonal state, which is studied by transpersonal psychology and which is found at the basis of all the great spiritual traditions.[6][7]

So, by the term 'mind' we imply this whole collection of energies — psyche, mind and spirituality — distinguishing between them to facilitate the teaching process.

Let us take a look at the techniques which help us attain peace of mind. Because of the holistic approach we are taking, these methods include peace of the body, peace of the heart and peace of mind.

Even relaxation, which we have introduced as a tool to create peace of the body, has emotional and mental repercussions. It spreads physical peace into the heart and mind.

The most important objective is to get to the point where we can go beyond and dissolve the fantasy of separation. We can achieve this by going beyond thought, the nature of which is to fragment, classify, divide. Thought, intelligence and reason are precious dialectical tools indispensable for daily life and our mental evolution. But at the same time thought is the big obstacle to evolution towards a holistic vision.

The best method for helping us to go beyond thought, while honouring its gifts, is meditation.

Meditation

Meditation has been defined in several ways. In fact this is a paradox, since it is a method that consists of sitting down and doing nothing. It is a return to oneself, to one's own body. In other words, it is about doing the opposite to what our industrial civilisation has conditioned us to do: to live outside ourselves, to direct all our activity towards the outside world, at the risk of reinforcing the fantasy of separation. This apparent non-activity is coupled with attention, observation and a mind open to everything that happens. The person who is meditating concentrates on a thought, an inner image, a sound or an object such as the flame of a candle. It doesn't matter what the object of concentration is; the important thing is the result: rambling thoughts die down and with them the ideas that separate the self from external objects, as well as separating the external objects themselves.

When we reach this state, the frontier between the 'I' and the external world dissolves and, among other effects, inner peace is regained.

Much criticism has been directed against this technique by people who are misinformed, misguided or have only read about meditation. The main criticism is that meditation alienates us from the material world at the heart of industrial civilisation.

In fact the reverse is true. Research done on the subject shows that meditation contributes directly to the improvement of the following functions: mental state, attention, memory, emotional equilibrium, synchronisation of the brainwaves of the two hemispheres of the brain, and productivity at work. Because it awakens our consciousness, meditation is the antidote to alienation.

To go within ourself for 20 minutes each morning and evening does not mean that we are isolating ourself from the outside world, but rather that we are learning to become more open, more conscious and less of an automaton — in other words, less alienated.

Above all, returning to our main topic, meditation helps to address the usual issues of daily life in a harmonious and peaceful way.

Conflicts continue but they are resolved without violence, with friendship and wisdom. A spirit of serenity takes over the conflict and allows us to find a solution within ourself and with others.

---

1. All human beings are an inseparable part of nature, upon which culture and human civilisation have been built.

2. Life on Earth is abundant and diverse. It is sustained by the unhindered functioning of natural systems which ensure the provision of energy, air, water and nutrients for all living creatures. Every manifestation of life on Earth is unique and essential and must therefore be respected and protected without regard to its apparent value to human beings.

Declaration of Human Responsibilities for Peace and Sustainable Development. Articles 2 and 3, Chapter I. United Nations University of Peace. Costa Rica, 1989.

All that we have said about meditation also applies to dance in its meditative forms, such as T'ai Chi. Originating from Taoism, this is still a national custom in China, and is practised by millions of Chinese in public places. Its essentials have been extracted to make it accessible to the west.

In Africa, Asia, Latin America and the Middle East, numerous ritual dances, through conscious trance, achieve similar effects — although research on an inter-cultural basis would be necessary to prove or disprove this last point.

In conclusion, meditative practices lead to what Abraham Maslow has called peak states or experiences, capable of unblocking and awakening the higher human and spiritual values, the same ones used by Gorbachev to motivate the Soviet worker.[10][11]

Figure 8 gives a summary of these values classified according to the human centres of energy (chakras), as described by yoga. Each of these centres, of which there are seven principal ones, corresponds to a different school of philosophy and psychology, all of which apparently contradict one another.[12] The centres can be used as an exclusive basis for the explanation and conciliation of opposing ideologies. This system could be an important instrument of peace, if detailed research were devoted to it.

Dualistic in appearance, our classification of values into constructive and destructive behaviours does not in any way imply that we view them in an absolute fashion. For example, we build a new building from the destruction of the old. The evolution of all that exists implies a continuous transformation of opposites into each other.

We can say the same thing about the hierarchy of values: it is only an appearance of experiences of different qualities at the level of existence. In fact, it is the manifestation in the human being of the same energy.

These concepts and techniques that enable us to awaken and develop the art of living in peace with ourselves are indistinguishable from those that enable us to live in peace with others. It is not only a training for a harmonious life in society, but is also a training that very often requires that we live with others. This is what we shall deal with in the next section.

References

1. Schulz, J.H. *Le Training Autogène*. Paris, PUF, 1965.

2. Caycedo, A. *L'Avenir de la Sophrologie*. Paris, Retz, 1979.

3. UNEP. *Personal Action Guide for the Earth*. Santa Monica, United Nations Environment Programme.

4. del Vasto, Lanza. *Technique de la Non Violence*. Paris, Denoel-Gonthier, 1971.

5. Brosse, Th. *La Conscience Energie*. Paris, Presence, 1979.

6. Weil, P. *Anthologie de l'Extase*. Paris, Question de . . . , Albin Michel, 1989.

7. Grof, S. *Transpersonal Psychology*. Audio cassette from 'Sounds True'.

8. See 12.

9. Found in the Christian and Tibetan Buddhist traditions.

10. Gorbachev, M. *Perestroika*. New York, Harper & Row, 1987/ Fontana (UK), 1988.

11. Maslow, A. *Towards a Psychology of Being*. Van Nost Reinhold, 1969.

12. Weil, P. *L'Homme Sans Frontières*. Paris, L'Espace Bleu, 1989. Pp 107-112.

Values and Behaviour

Classification of values	Values	Behaviour	
		Constructive	Destructive
Transpersonal	union the sacred wisdom grace bliss fulfilment wholeness	harmony non-duality	division judgement anger
Knowledge	knowing clarity truth justice	meditation reflection self-discovery equanimity	ignorance lying hiding
Inspiration	creativity beauty	imagination intuition trust creativity openness	closedness
Love	altruism humanism harmony tenderness	understanding empathy help	rancour selfishness resentment
Power	equanimity autonomy	cooperation freedom of speech	domination dependence
Sensuality	pleasure	sharing	possessiveness attachment
Security	freedom of body health existence basic well-being	respect non-violence courage peace	violence aggression allowing killing infection pollution

Figure 8

METHODS OF EDUCATION

We recall that the fundamental theory of the process of the destruction of peace (in the long-term section of the last module) and of the process of the creation of the vicious circle of compulsive repetition characteristic of the 'neurosis of paradise lost' (short-term section), provokes a sufficiently strong motivation to search for a means of escaping the vicious circle and to learn the techniques which foster the attainment of inner peace.

In fact the description in the previous section is full of suggested methods. We return to the subject only to mention which methods to develop in the short-, medium- and long-term programmes.

Short-term

In the Art of Living in Peace workshop, the educational methods are divided up in the following manner, in line with the scheme mentioned previously.

— Being at peace with oneself (inner ecology) —

1. *Preliminary session*
Initial motivation of participants and creating a warm and happy atmosphere (dancing and questions).

2. *Past, present and future of humanity*
Use of brainstorming to make an assessment of past, present and future, and also to create an awareness of the enormous gap that separates human ideals of peace from reality, now or in the past.

3. *Obstacles to peace*
Brief summary of the fundamental theory of the process of the destruction of peace.

4. *Being at peace with oneself* (inner ecology)

● The origin of the neurosis of paradise lost.
    Theory and dramatisation.

● Peace of the body.
    Relaxation and nutritional advice.

● Peace of the heart.
    Becoming aware of destructive emotions.
    Visualising a new constructive project.
    Psychotherapies.
    Heart qualities and how to awaken them.

● Peace of mind.
    How can we move beyond fragmentation?
    Dancing and life.
    Meditation.
    Peak experiences.
    Towards a scale of 'constructive' values.

Medium- and long-term

The above programme can be undertaken in detail, with the help of good professionals or masters of the various disciplines mentioned in the text (relaxation, yoga, meditation, T'ai Chi), health and nutrition counsellors, and therapists of various persuasions.

One could also add some of the new cooperative games[1] and peace games that have recently been created by the Findhorn Community.[2]

In addition to the psychotherapies, a long-term programme can be an excellent opportunity for initiation into the spiritual traditions to which the Declarations of Venice and Vancouver refer.

The art of living in peace with others

The contemporary 'normosis'

We have already seen how a lack of harmony causes us to create a society that is violent, pathological and in its turn pathogenic in its relation to the individual, to such an extent that we find we are prisoners in a closed system where nobody knows where things start: in the individual or in society.

One could even say that the majority of opinions, attitudes and behaviours about which there is a general consensus and which dictate what is 'normal', in reality lead us to a 'normosis', because in effect these agreements are social pressures which force the individual, in one way or another, to 'adapt' to abnormal rules.

Among these pathogenic and aberrant consensuses we find the concept of 'fair war', which even has solid support in law. Once war has been legally declared, we acquire the right to kill all our enemies. In the name of this 'normal' principle, we train all the young men of the world — this youth which basically desires only peace — to kill their fellow humans, during their 'normally' obligatory period of military service.

A similar consensus existed in the past concerning duelling to avenge one's damaged honour. This practice is today considered illegal, outmoded and even ridiculous. When will war be outlawed, as duelling was? Isn't it in fact a collective duel? Will the world take this same evolutionary step with regard to violence and war?

It is this that we are working towards. To that end, we must help humanity escape from its 'normosis', to develop the full awareness that will prevent people from adapting to consensi and rules which are in fact pathological, even though they are statistically 'normal'.

In this respect it is just as important to work on the

social level as on the individual level, and if possible both simultaneously.

The three social manifestations of energy

In the area of society, characterised by the social sciences, we have quite a number of research projects and programmes of action concerned with war, violence and peace, although this isn't the place to go into them in great detail. There are available in the educational field some excellent summaries of this work, especially relating to the social and international levels.[345]

We are going to classify them according to our non-fragmented model of energy according to which it manifests on the social level in three forms.

● *Culture*, which corresponds on an energy level to human and universal intelligence, is the domain of anthropology and legal studies.

It consists of the sum total of the consensi, opinions, attitudes, feelings, perspectives, concepts, stereotypes, prejudices and laws of any given society. It is culture that dictates the habits and behaviour of this society. It is expressed through art in its various forms, through philosophy, scientific knowledge, spiritual values, and it is passed on through social institutions such as the family, schools and public and private organisations.

● *Society* corresponds on the energy level to human and universal life and its principal science is sociology.

Society consists of the sum total of relationships, interactions and communications between individuals, groups and institutions. It is expressed by means of or within social institutions such as the family, schools, universities, businesses, and governmental and non-governmental organisations.

● *Economy* of material goods, which corresponds on the energy level to the human body and universal matter, is the domain of the economic sciences.

It refers to the production, distribution and consumption or use of habitat or territory, of food, clothing and wealth of any kind, including money and its circulation. It functions through the individual worker or private and public organisations.

We shall now, for each of these groups, which are closely linked, describe the various methods and educational techniques that have been recommended as solutions during the course of the past forty years.

We can distinguish three types of education for social and international peace: *cultural education for peace, social education for peace* and *economic education for peace*. Since there have been a considerable number of suggested solutions, we limit ourselves here to a simple listing of them accompanied by some essential comments.

Cultural education for peace

On the level on which we have defined it, it is possible to draw attention to numerous educational initiatives aimed at changing concepts, opinions, feelings and values. As Johan Galtung has shown,[6] the goal is to transform the values relating to the world we reject and that we no longer want, into those of a world we prefer.

The main educational techniques currently recommended or used are as follows.

— The teaching and promulgation of the International Charter of Human Rights[7]

A look at the ratifications of the principal international tools for promoting human rights[8] shows us to what extent the efforts of the United Nations have put values linked with human rights onto the agenda of almost every country in the world. To a large extent this is the result of a huge educational campaign.

Unesco recently published[9] a guide for teaching human rights at all levels and in all the different kinds of education. In his commentary on this G.B. Kutukdjian gives a general idea of 'the great lessons to be drawn from the educational work of these past years' and states that 'perhaps the study of human rights is not a supplementary subject to add to the curriculum, because in essence it is reflection and research . . . on concrete and tangible social relationships. Henceforth the teaching of human rights — training for democracy (rights, duties and obligations) — will become education for freedom and solidarity.'[10]

This Unesco publication contains some valuable pointers for programmes and educational principles which can be used as a basis for teaching human rights at university level, in primary or secondary education, and in community education. It also contains a bibliography on human rights education.

— Cultural education for peace through the mass media

The press, newspapers, magazines, radio, television and advertising are, as we well know, vehicles of enormous power for the promulgation of values of peace.

Numerous studies have been carried out into the role of the mass media in encouraging violence in the world. In his introduction to the Unesco publication *Violence and Terror in the Mass Media* [12] Georges Gerbner states that violence and terror in the mass media give social relationships a conflicting image; they show how force can be used to control, isolate, dominate, provoke or destroy. Some of the research cited shows that the percentage of violent content has increased considerably in television programmes and now affects more than half of all programmes.

The studies carried out on the educational role that the mass media should play are already numerous. There is a summary of them in a Unesco publication called *Media Education*.[12] In fact the mass media constitute a fourth power in society, the scale of which we are only just beginning to become aware. To state that it should take on an educational role because of its power is not enough. If we are to believe Michel Souchon, in his conclusion to the above-mentioned publication, extremely strong trends mark the history of relationships between the educational world and that of the mass media. Among these trends he points out the use of the media for purposes of entertainment, the restriction and uneven distribution of financial resources, and outmoded techniques of education which are not well-suited to the demands of the media. Reconciliation between education and the media is possible, however,[13] and there are indications that it is happening in several countries. That, at least, is desirable.

— Other educational approaches relating to a culture of peace

The subject is so vast that here we can only touch lightly on the various perspectives, each one of which, nevertheless, merits a detailed presentation and which are in fact the objects of educational studies and practices. Among others, we mention:

- *Libraries* dedicated to peace and the introduction of the subject into existing libraries.
- *Law education* relating to peace, in the law schools.
- The study and promulgation of a *global history of peace* which would be a means of balancing the

obvious tendency of school textbooks to provide only facts relating to battles, victories and defeats.

● The development of an *organisational holistic cultural movement* in business and in governmental and non-governmental organisations, starting with the various branches of the United Nations. This culture would take into consideration human beings, production and sufficiency that is indispensable for peace to come about.

● The increase of the *international pen-pal movement* for young people all over the world.

● The education of *soldiers for peace*, beginning with the introduction in military academies of courses on the role of the military in the preservation of peace and strategies for transforming military service into civil service in countries which constitute economic or political communities, such as the European Community, on condition that the same is done in every country in the world.[14]

● *Education for disarmament* is a related aspect. The World Congress on Education for Disarmament lists the essential points of this kind of education and recommends that students develop a critical judgement regarding steps taken to reduce armaments and to eliminate war as 'an internationally acceptable practice'.[15]

All human beings inseparably belong to the human family and depend on one another for their existence, well-being and development.

Declaration of Human Responsibilities for Peace and Sustainable Development. Article 4, Chapter II. University of Peace, Costa Rica, 1989.

Social education for peace

The establishment of peace on the social level depends not only on individual education for peace, as we discussed earlier, but also on direct action on human interpersonal relationships, between different groups and nations.

To this end several methods have been developed, especially after the second world war. We mention a few:

● *Group dynamics* in its various forms: T-groups, encounter groups, intergroup workshops, leading of meetings, management leadership training, pscyho-sociological intervention. The main purpose of these techniques is to identify and work on, in a real-life situation, obstacles to communication and causes of conflict. Set in motion by the studies of Kurt Lewin and the work of the National Training Laboratories of Bethel (NTL), there are now innumerable variations of this method.

● Having identical objectives are *psychodrama, sociodrama, role-playing* and *sociometry* created by J.L. Moreno. The applications of these to social education for peace are considerable.

● *Non-competitive games and sports* stimulate cooperation, as we discussed earlier.

● *Peace strategy games,* simulations of international peace strategies, allow us to forecast to a certain extent the reactions of enemies; for example taking the initiative to make an important unilateral reduction in weapons can encourage the other side to do the same, as has already been the case.

● *Martial arts* such as aikido and Japanese judo foster a calm state of mind and respect for one's opponent as well as an awareness of what is happening on an energy level within oneself and with others.

● *On the political level* an attempt to create peace could be developed through the organisation of conferences and meetings where politicians could together make a study of what unites them beyond their ideological differences.

● *On the religious level* these last thirty years have been a witness to ecumenical meetings, conferences and seminars of remarkable quality, contributing to and fostering reconciliation and understanding between the representatives of the various spiritual traditions.

What is important about all the above methods is that we re-learn respect for the essence of each of our fellow human beings.

Economic education for peace

As long as there is poverty, hunger, disease, infant mortality, overpopulation and the abandonment of millions of children in the streets, it will not be possible to attain peace either in our consciousness, or in our national or international relationships.

In fact, for reasons that we are unable to discuss here but which originate in the fantasy of separation and possessiveness, existing economic systems have only partially solved this problem.

In order for there to be economic education for peace, we need an economic theory of peace that takes into consideration individual, social and ecological concomitances — in other words, a new holistic economy which integrates and goes beyond the positive contributions of current economic systems.

It will take interdisciplinary teams working both theoretically and experimentally to create that theory and to formulate recommendations for the various countries of the world based on research into economic solutions and taking into account the five 'E's recommended by Pierre Danserau, namely: ecology, ethology, economy in its true sense, ethnology and ethics.[16]

In the meantime, we can only concentrate on the following approaches to economic education for peace:

● To continue to publish critical analyses of the war-fostering aspects of current economic systems. There are studies which meet this need.[17] It goes without saying that all educational methods can be used to this end. Johan Galtung, for example, suggests the use of dramatisation to play out the effects of the different socio-economic systems.

● To promulgate and encourage movements and attitudes likely to remedy the current situation. Among these we can mention:

— *Voluntary simplicity*, which is a movement sparked by E.F. Schumacher in his book *Small is Beautiful*[18] and amplified under this title by Duane Elgin.[19] The originator of this expression, Richard Gregg, defined it in the following way:[20] 'Voluntary simplicity applies to internal and external conditions alike. It involves purity of intention, sincerity and honesty towards oneself, as well as the avoidance of outer complications, of having lots of trivial possessions as our main purpose for living. It means organising our energy and our desires, partly restricting ourselves in some aspects of life to ensure a greater abundance of life in other ways. This implies a conscious organisation of our life towards a meaningful goal.'

It seems that several million people in the developed countries are practising, more or less completely, this new way of living. But in the still-developing countries, the opposite problem presents itself, that of basic well-being.

— *Basic well-being.* To define basic well-being is not simple because it depends on the economic level of each population. It isn't the same for a European as for an Indian.

Nevertheless, we can agree on one thing. All human beings need wholesome and sufficient nourishment to maintain their health, and they need shelter against bad weather and clothes to protect them from extremes of temperature.

Shall we get there one day? The answer belongs to the future.

REFERENCES

1. Lefèvre, N. Dale. *New Games for the Whole Family.* New York, Perigee, 1988.

2. Ibid.

3. Unesco. *Education for International Cooperation and Peace at the Primary School Level.* Paris, Unesco, 1983.

4. Wulf, C. et al. *Handbook of Peace Education.* Frankfurt, IPRA, 1974.

5. Boulding, Elise. *The Child and Non-Violent Social Change.* Ibid. pp 101-135.

6. Galtung, Johan. *On Peace Education.* Ibid. pp 169.

7. United Nations. *Human Rights — The International Charter of Human Rights.* New York, United Nations, 1988.

8. *State of Ratification of the Main International Instruments Relating to Human Rights on January 1, 1990.* Greenwood Press/Unesco, 1982, Appendix I.

9. *Teaching Human Rights.* Paris, Unesco, 1986, Vol. V.

10. Kutukdjian, G.B. Commentary in ibid. pp 1-2.

11. Gerner, Georges. *Violence and Terror in the Media.* Paris,

Unesco, Studies and Information Documents, no. 102, 1989, Introduction.

12. Unesco. *Media Education.* Paris, Unesco, 1984.

13. Souchon, Michel. *Education and the Mass Media: Contradictions and Convergences.* In *Media Education.* Paris, Unesco, 1985.

14. Conclusions of the *Soldiers for Peace* Seminar held in April 1990 at the City of Peace Foundation, International Holistic University of Brasilia (not published).

15. *Unesco Yearbook on Peace and Conflict Studies.* Paris, Unesco, 1987, pp 118-121.

16. Danserau, Pierre. *La Terre des Hommes et le Paysage Intérieur.* Quebec, Lemeac, 1973, pp 143 ff.

17. See for example the study by Jurgen Markstahler, Volker Wagner and Dieter Sanghaas on 'Structural Dependence and Underdevelopment'. In *Handbook of Peace Education* (see no. 4), pp 185 ff.

18. Schumacher, E.F. *Small is Beautiful.* London, Vintage, 1993.

19. Elgin, Duane. *Voluntary Simplicity.* New Jersey, William Morrow, 1988.

20. See 12, pp 15-40.

METHODS OF EDUCATION

Short-term

We present here an outline of the techniques used in our Art of Living in Peace workshop, as far as they concern living in peace with others.

We shall not go into them in great detail as we do not want to detract from the effects that people experience from encountering them for the first time and also because some of the techniques must be undertaken by educators themselves so that they can understand their importance and the way they work. Just reading about them is not recommended and would not have any effect.

— Peace with others (social ecology)

- The process of the destruction of social ecology.
- Brief reminder of the process of destruction of inner harmony and its repercussions on social harmony. The destruction of peace on the cultural, social and economic level.
- Experience of group dynamics with regard to concepts and prejudices: what it is that divides the group and what unites it.

— Rebuilding peace in society

On the economic level (reading and discussion of texts)

- Basic well-being
- Voluntary simplicity
- New professional motivation

On the social level

- The causes of war and peace (discussion of texts)
- Education for peace (comments)

- Spiritual interaction (group experience)
- Humankind around the planet (visualisation with sound-track)

On the cultural level

- The International Charter of Human Rights (reading and discussion)
- Universal values (review and comments)

Medium- and long-term

The basic text for this module makes numerous suggestions. Collaboration with psycho-sociologists, sociologists, anthropologists and economists will without doubt be of great assistance.

The same plan as indicated for a short-term programme can be followed.

Here are some suggested sources for research and additional consultation:

Amadou Mahtar M'Bow et al. *Consensus and Peace*. Paris, Unesco, 1980.

Didier, Pierre François. *Guide Pratique de la Paix Mondiale*. Paris, Marval, 1985. This contains a source of inspiration in the form of 38 'levers' for peace.

Ferencz, B.B. & Keyes Jr, Ken. *Planethood: The Key to Your Future*. Preface by Robert Muller. Love Line Books (US), 1991.

Muller, Robert. *Nouvelle Génèse. Vers un Spiritualité Globale*. Quebec, Knowlton, Les Editions Universelles de Verseau, 1990.

Marquier-Dumont. *Le Défi de l'Humanité*. Quebec, Knowlton, Les Editions Universelles de Verseau, 1987.

Unesco Yearbook on Peace and Conflict Studies. Paris, Unesco, yearly.

The art of living in peace with the environment

Human nature and the nature of the environment

The environment is an expression of universal energy. As human beings we are an integral part of it. Moreover, we are made of this energy and as a consequence we integrate it within ourselves.

As we saw previously, the loss of this notion of inseparability between humans and nature lies at the root of our destruction of the environment.

To train others in the art of living in peace with nature involves before all else re-establishing in human beings this holistic vision of their unseverable connection with nature.

Starting with the personal egocentric consciousness, broadening out into anthropocentric social consciousness and moving on to a geocentric planetary consciousness, humankind will have to discover a transpersonal and universal cosmic consciousness.

As we suggested above, the non-fragmentary theory of energy allows us to provide models for understanding the nature of things, to clearly classify the great problems that afflict the human race, as well as to propose solutions for recovering our lost peace.

Towards a method of ecological education

This non-fragmentary theory of energy also offers the possibility, on the level of the relationship between humans and their environment, of establishing a method of education which helps humankind become aware that its own nature and the nature of the universe are in essence the same.

The immediate consequence of this is that we will come to the obvious conclusion that all thought followed by actions that harm the environment will directly or indirectly, in the short or long term, affect ourselves or our descendants. It makes us co-responsible for the preservation of the environment.

This, then, is clearly the essential objective of a method of ecological education, which would be part of a curriculum that follows the three main manifestations of energy. Although we discussed these earlier, we shall summarise them here.

The three forms of manifestation of energy in the natural world are *matter, life* and *information.* As they are varying manifestations of *one energy* they are obviously indivisible to the extent that they are represented within each other, as in a hologram.

Moreover, we can say that there is life in matter, composed of solid, liquid, fiery and gaseous elements, according to so-called physical laws, which are its informational aspect. In this sense matter is intelligent . . . .

In the same way, we can state that life originates from matter and obeys what we call biological laws. Life implies the existence of information; everything takes place as if life itself were intelligent and wise. Information does not evade this three-in-one aspect since its transmission depends on physical systems in all the processes of communication and communication itself is a vital process that finds its ultimate expression in love. Information is the expression of laws of wisdom which are part of the implicate order of the universe, as David Bohm describes.[1] In this sense the nature of the universe and the universe of nature would be a thought full of love. Here we reach the frontier where perhaps poetry and the real world merge and where the universe takes on a psychological aspect, although without implying an anthropomorphic projection. On the contrary, humankind would only be a reflection of this psycho-cosmological aspect of the universe; if there is any projection, it would be that of nature within humans.

So, let us again take the three-in-one concept of energy and examine its educational forms for giving humans the opportunity to become aware in themselves of their fundamental inseparability from the environment. This implies, on the epistemological level, the acceptance of the idea of the indivisibility of physics, biology and psychology.

In the same way, inner ecology, social ecology and planetary ecology all constitute only one ecology.

The recognition by a human being that he is part of the same process that defines the universe, enhances his self-image and allows him to transcend egoism, which is the principal threat to his own long-term interests and to the environment and, in consequence, to his future.

Vancouver Declaration on Survival into the 21st Century. Unesco, 15 September, 1989.

The most direct way of achieving this purpose is to make each human being aware of the correspondence that exists between his own structure and vital or psychic systems, and the structure and vital or cybernetic systems of the universe. In other words, the correspondence between his inner world and his outer world, between himself as subject and the universe as object.

It is obvious that educators will themselves have to be deeply convinced of this correspondence and of the kind of illusion in which the majority of humankind is caught, before wanting to encourage such a vision in others.

The method of ecological education will also have to educate trainees or students in how to preserve the environment.

Now we shall look at these three aspects of ecological education, namely: ecological education about matter, ecological education about life and ecological education about information.

The method of ecological education

As recommended by Pierre Dansereau, it is sensible to start with matter in relation to any analysis of ecosystems, in the sense of so-called inorganic matter.[2] In his ecosystem model this renowned ecologist distinguishes the following six levels : mineral, vegetable, herbivorous animals, carnivorous animals, the level of investment and that of control.

In the energetic flow minerals are absorbed by plants; plants are eaten by herbivores, who themselves provide food for carnivores; moreover, at every level we can notice investments by plants, animals and human beings aimed at accumulating reserves; on the latter level we find will and planning which corresponds to Teilhard de Chardin's noosphere.[3]

So we start with a method of ecological education in relation to matter. Our experience tells us that the best way to awaken a consciousness of the non-separation between humans and inorganic matter is to use every possible form of demonstration of the correspondence between the human body and matter. It is also possible to help people understand and become aware of the correspondence between the 'outer' and the 'inner', in relation to the earth, the soil, water, fire in the form of light and heat, the atmosphere and the air, and even the space-energy of which everything is ultimately made. This can be done by theoretical studies, research activities and visualisation.

The same methods are applied to plant and animal life.

The concept of an organic macrocosm recaptures the rhythms of life. These rhythms can help human beings reintegrate with nature and restore their relationship with others in space and in time.

Vancouver Declaration on Survival into the 21st Century. Unesco, 15 September, 1989.

It is relatively easy for students to understand that there is life in both themselves and the universe and that it is all one life. A comparative analysis of human, plant and animal evolution encourages and reinforces this work.

Relating information and the intelligence directing the ecosystems by means of human intelligence and thought and the demonstration of the existence of a wisdom immanent in humans and nature can initially give rise to certain theoretical or even ideological objections. That is why the demonstration must be based on a rigorous observation of facts, leaving each student free to make his or her own analogies and conclusions in relation to this subject. For example, deep reflection on a seed, on the blueprint for a tree that does not yet exist, and comparison with a mental project, that is, the idea of a hut which does not yet exist, constitutes among other methods quite a good means of creating awareness of this subject.[4]

The second aspect to consider is creating awareness of the need to protect the environment. Certain universities are taking a growing interest in this question and their programmes will serve as a source of inspiration. In addition, the report of the World Commission on Environment and Development, known as the Brundtland Report, is also a source of inspiration for curricula,[5] while Unesco's 'Man and the Biosphere' (MAB) programme provides information that can be used in formulating courses and educational and training methods.[6]

But as our study is centred on peace, the aim of ecological education for peace is obviously not to train spe-
cialists in the environment, but to make the majority of
educators — and through them the population of the
Earth — aware of their contribution and individual responsibility with regard to the environment. That is why our first
section of suggestions relating to the diminution or even
dissolution of the fantasy of separation is so important.
They are effective in awakening an attitude of profound
respect towards the planet, which we begin to perceive
as an extension of ourselves, to which we are linked by an
umbilical cord, as invisible as the air which links us to it.

What is needed, then, is to complete this process of
creating awareness with recommendations on the effective contribution that each individual can bring to this
field. Lists of specific actions exist in numerous publications.[78] The subject of nutrition can be a good starting point
for demonstrating the relationship between the environment and ourselves.[9 10]

The Declaration of Human Responsibility for Peace and
Sustainable Development issued by the United Nations'
University of Peace is a document which should be made
an obligatory part of this type of curriculum, for it provides
a theoretical and ethical support not only within the scope
of this current module, but also for the principal ideas
which we have developed throughout this book.[11]

REFERENCES

1. Bohm, David. *The Undivided Universe*. London, Routledge.

2. Dansereau, Pierre. *La Terre des Hommes et le Paysage Intérieur*. Ottawa, Lemeac, 1973, pp 84-89.

3. Teilhard de Chardin, Pierre. *Le Phénomène Humain*. Paris, Seuil, 1955.

4. We can also compare the blueprint within the seed and that of the spermatozoa and the ovum. The idea of non-separation between individual consciousness and universal or cosmic consciousness has developed within a new branch of psychology: transpersonal psychology. This has brought about numerous meetings between physicists on the one hand and psychologists and representatives of the great spiritual traditions on the other.

5. *Our Common Future*. Oxford/New York, Oxford University Press, 1987.

6. *Man Belongs to the Earth*. Paris, Unesco, 1988, pp 115-126.

7. *Guide d'Action Personnelle pour la Terre*. New York, Projet de transmission du programme de l'environment des Nations Unies, 1989.

8. Didier, Pierre François. *Guide Pratique de la Paix Mondiale*. Paris, Marval, 1985, pp 70-77.

9. Robbins, John. *Diet For a New America*. Stillpoint, 1990.

10. Desbrosses, Philippe. *Le Krach Alimentaire*. Préface de l'Abbé Pierre. Editions du Rocher, 1988.

11. *Declaration of Human Responsibilities for Peace and Sustainable Development*. United Nations' University of Peace, Costa Rica, 1989.

METHODS OF EDUCATION

Short-term

The Art of Living in Peace workshop, the seminar devised by the International Holistic University of Brasilia, part of the City of Peace Foundation, constitutes, on the level of ecological education for peace, a means of providing people with permanent motivation for taking personal and effective action with regard to the environment.

This is its basic outline:

Peace with nature (planetary ecology)

- *The process of the destruction of the environment* (verbal presentation).

- *Re-establishment of harmony with the environment* (verbal presentation).

- *Peace with nature.*

- *Matter.* Journey into external and internal matter. Visualisation on the themes of earth, water, fire, air and space-energy.

- *Life, outer and inner.* Where do we come from? Where are we? Where are we going? A real-life experience of nature, done in pairs.

- *Information. Outer and inner intelligence.* Concentration and reflection on a seed and on the process of thought.

- *The dissolution of the fantasy of separation.* Summary of the phases of dissolution (verbal description).

- *Project for contributing personally to peace with the environment.* It is important that this part of the training ends with a firm resolution to make a contribution to peace and to ecology, and that for each person this resolution is reinforced and accompanied by an individual plan of action, rooted in daily life.

● *What I have done and what I am currently doing for peace and the environment.* Each person makes a list of past and present actions.

● *What I can and want to do in the immediate future and in the medium term for peace with the environment.* Brainstorming in small groups, followed by final decisions. Visualisation of a specific situation in the near future.

Medium- and long-term

Exhibition on the environment organised by the students, grass roots research in groups, invitation to ecologists to come and speak, films and videos, group excursions and trips, in addition to everything that we have previously mentioned on the subject of organising a curriculum based on this module.

As far as the individual practical action is concerned, Art of Living in Peace circles, composed of about ten students at most, provide a framework for help and mutual support which helps to enhance each person's efforts.

APPENDICES

READING OF THE DECLARATION OF HUMAN RESPONSIBILITIES FOR PEACE AND SUSTAINABLE DEVELOPMENT

By Lic. Rodrigo Madrigal Nieto,
Minister of Foreign Affairs*, Costa Rica

Introduction to the reading

I will follow the advice of our dear Monsignor Troyo and, instead of adhering to protocol, I wish to call you all dear friends and to give a very special greeting to His Holiness the Dalai Lama, who honours and inspires us with his visit.

In effect, the Government has prepared a Declaration to be presented later to the United Nations with the hope that it will be accepted by this high organisation as a norm of living for humanity. It is entitled Declaration of Human Responsibilities for Peace and Sustainable Development.

This is only a first draft of this purpose, so that people like you, patient and wilful architects of the cause of peace, can add your reflections and together we can perfect the document for this purpose of illuminating the path of humanity, for this and future generations.

The Declaration would state thus:

Declaration of Human Responsibilities for Peace and Sustainable Development

Preamble

Considering that both the report of the World Commission on Environment and Development[1] and the United Nations Environmental Perspective to the Year 2000 and Beyond[2] have recognised the imminent peril threatening the existence of the Earth as a result of war and environmental destruction;

Recognising that the world has been evolving from a group

---

* As the Foreign Minister states in his introduction, he read a preliminary version of the Declaration during the Closing Ceremony of the Conference. The version published herein is the final version, which has incorporated amendments suggested by the Conference participants. This final version was presented to the General Assembly of the United Nations by the Government of Costa Rica on October 11, 1989 and circulated in all of the UN languages as Document A/44/626.

[1] Accepted by General Assembly resolution 42/187 of 11 December 1987.

[2] Accepted by General Assembly resolution 42/186 of 11 December 1987.

of separate communities towards interdependence and the beginnings of a world community, a process reflecting global concerns, common goals and shared ideals;

Recalling that, according to the Universal Declaration of Human Rights, recognition of the inherent dignity and of the equal and inalienable human rights of all members of the human family is the foundation of freedom, justice and peace in the world;

Considering the aspirations of all the members of the human family to realise their potential to the maximum through the cultural, social, political and economic development of individuals and of communities, recognised in the Declaration on the Right to Development[3] as an inalienable human right;

Recognising the necessity of ensuring the full and equal participation of women and men in the decision-making process related to the promotion of peace and development;

Bearing in mind that the international community has proclaimed that people have a sacred right to peace[4] and has recommended that national and international organisations should promote peace;[5]

Observing that the international community has recognised the fundamental right of human beings to live in an environment of equality that permits a life of dignity and well-being;[6]

Bearing in mind the challenge posed by the growing imbalances in the dynamic relationship between population, resources and the environment;

Considering that the General Assembly has established that all human rights and fundamental freedoms are indivisible and interdependent;[7]

Aware that the attainment of those rights has been recognised as being the responsibility of individuals as well as of States;[8]

Concerned because the efforts of human society thus far have not been sufficient to achieve the full recognition of those rights;

Considering that the United Nations has emphasised that wars begin in the minds and through the actions of human

---

[3] General Assembly resolution 41/128 of December 1986.

[4] Declaration on the Right of Peoples to Peace, General Assembly resolution 39/11 of 12 November 1984.

[5] Declaration on the Preparation of Societies for Life in Peace, General Assembly resolution 33/73 of 15 December 1978.

[6] Report of the United Nations Conference on the Human Environment (the Stockholm Declaration), 16 June 1972.

[7] General Assembly resolution 37/199 of 18 December 1982.

[8] See World Charter for Nature: General Assembly resolution 37/7 of 28 October 1982, and resolution 38/124 of 16 December 1983.

beings[9] and that the threats to continuing development and the conservation of the environment arise from diverse but inter-related forms of human behaviour;[10]

Bearing in mind that the General Assembly has determined that, in order to ensure the survival of natural systems and an adequate level of living for all, human activity should be reori-ented towards the goal of sustainable development;[11]

Considering that the present generation, having reached a crossroads where new challenges and decisions must be faced, bears the immediate responsibility for its own development and for the survival of future generations, to consciously constitute a single world, just, peaceful and based on cooperation with nature;

Convinced, therefore, that there is an urgent need for a greater awareness of the unity of life and of the special char-acter of each of the expressions of life, and for a more profound human sense of responsibility and a reorientation of human thoughts, feelings and actions;

Considering that this Declaration can contribute to the achievement of this reorientation and can inspire many practi-cal applications at the level of the individual, the family and the community as well as at the national and international levels;

In accordance with all the foregoing considerations, the Government of Costa Rica offers the present Declaration of Human Responsibilities for Peace and Sustainable Development as an instrument for reflection and commitment.

Chapter I
Unity of the World

Article 1. Everything which exists is part of an interdependent uni-verse. All living beings depend on one another for their existence, well-being and development.

Article 2. All human beings are an inseparable part of nature, upon which culture and human civilisation have been built.

Article 3. Life on Earth is abundant and diverse. It is sustained by the unhindered functioning of natural systems which ensure the provision of energy, air, water and nutrients for all living crea-tures. Every manifestation of life on Earth is unique and essential

---

[9] Declaration on the Preparation of Societies for Life in Peace: General Assembly resolution 33/73 of 15 December 1978; Constitution of the United Nations Educational, Scientific and Cultural Organisation, pre-amble, paragraph 1.

[10] General Assembly resolutions 37/7 of 28 October 1982: 42/186 of 11 December 1987 and 42/187 of 11 December 1987.

[11] General Assembly resolutions 42/186 and 42/187 of 11 December 1987.

and must therefore be respected and protected without regard to its apparent value to human beings.

Chapter II
Unity of the Human Family

Article 4. All human beings inseparably belong to the human family and depend on one another for their existence, well-being and development. Every human being is a unique expression and manifestation of life and has a personal contribution to make to life on Earth. Each human being has fundamental and inalienable rights and freedoms, without distinction of race, colour, sex, language, religion, political or other opinion, national or social origin, economic status or any other social situation.

Article 5. All human beings have the same basic needs and the same fundamental aspirations for their fulfilment. All individuals are the beneficiaries of the right to development, the purpose of which is to promote attainment of the full potential of each person.

Chapter III
The Alternatives Facing Humanity, and Universal Responsibility

Article 6. Responsibility is an inherent aspect of any relation in which human beings are involved. This capacity to act responsibly in a conscious, independent, unique and personal manner is an inalienable creative quality of every human being. There is no limit to its scope or depth other than that established by each person for himself. The more it is acted upon and put into practice, the more it will grow and become strengthened.

Article 7. Of all living beings, human beings have the unique capacity to decide consciously whether to protect or harm the quality and conditions of life on Earth. In reflecting on the fact that they belong to the natural world and occupy a special position as participants in the evolution of natural processes, individuals can develop, on the basis of altruism, compassion, and love, a sense of universal responsibility toward the world as an integral whole, toward the protection of nature, and toward the promotion of the highest evolutionary potential, with a view to creating those conditions which will enable them to achieve the highest level of spiritual and material well-being.

Article 8. At this critical time in history, human choices are crucial. In directing their actions toward the attainment of progress in society, human beings have frequently forgotten that they belong to the natural world, to an indivisible human family, and have overlooked their basic needs for a healthy life. Excessive consumption, abuse of the environment, and aggression between peoples have brought the natural processes of the Earth to a critical stage which threatens their survival. By reflecting on these issues, individuals will be able to discern their responsibility and, upon this basis, reorient their conduct toward peace and sustainable development.

Chapter IV
Reorientation Toward Peace and Sustainable Development

Article 9. When individuals recognise that all forms of life are unique and essential, that all human beings are the beneficiaries of the right to development, and that both peace and violence have their origins in the consciousness of persons, a sense of responsibility to act and think in a peaceful manner will develop. Through this peaceful consciousness, individuals will understand the nature of those conditions which are necessary for their well-being and development.

Article 10. Human beings who become conscious of their sense of responsibility toward the human family, the environment they inhabit, and of the need to think and act in a peaceful manner will realise their obligation to act in a way that is consistent with the observance of and respect for inherent human rights and will ensure that their consumption of resources is in keeping with the satisfaction of the basic needs of all.

Article 11. When members of the human family recognise that they are responsible to themselves and to present and future generations for the conservation of the planet, as protectors of the natural world and promoters of its continued development, they will realise their obligation to act in a rational manner in order to ensure the sustainability of life.

Article 12. Human beings have a continuing responsibility when setting up, taking part in or representing social units, corporations, and institutions, whether private or public. In addition, all such entities have a responsibility to promote peace and sustainability, and to put into practice the educational goals which are conducive to that end. These goals include fostering the consciousness of the interdependence of human beings among themselves and with nature, and awareness of the universal responsibility of individuals to solve the problems which they have engendered through their attitudes and actions, in a manner that is consistent with the protection of human rights and fundamental freedoms.

Let us be faithful to the privilege of our responsibility.

Venice Declaration

Final Communiqué of the Symposium

Science and the Boundaries of Knowledge
The Prologue of our Cultural Past

Venice, 7 March 1986

The participants in the symposium 'Science and the Boundaries of Knowledge: The Prologue of our Cultural Past', organised by Unesco in collaboration with the Giorgio Cini Foundation (Venice, 3-7 March 1986), in a spirit of open-mindedness and enquiry concerning today's values, have agreed on the following points:

1. We are witnessing a very important revolution in the field of science brought about by basic science (in particular by developments in physics and biology), by the upheavals it has wrought in logic, in epistemology and in everyday life through its technological applications. We note at the same time, however, a significant gap between a new world view emerging from the study of natural systems and the values that continue to prevail in philosophy, in the human and social sciences and in the life of modern society, values largely based on mechanistic determinism, positivism, or nihilism. We believe that this discrepancy is harmful and indeed dangerous for the very survival of our species.

2. Scientific knowledge, on its own impetus, has reached the point where it can begin a dialogue with other forms of knowledge. In this sense, and while recognising the fundamental differences between science and tradition, we see them as complementary rather than in contradiction. This new and mutually enriching exchange between science and the different traditions of the world opens the door to a new vision of humanity, and even to a new rationalism, which could lead to a new metaphysical perspective.

3. While not wishing to attempt a global approach, nor to establish a closed system of thought, nor to invent a new utopia, we recognise the pressing need for truly transdisciplinary research through a dynamic exchange between the natural sciences, the social sciences, art and tradition. It could be said that this

transdisciplinary mode is inherent in our brain through the dynamic interaction of its two hemispheres. Joint investigation of nature and of the imagination, of the universe and of man, might thus bring us closer to reality and enable us better to meet the various challenges of our time.

4. The conventional way of teaching science by a linear presentation of knowledge masks the divorce between today's science and world views which are outdated. We stress the need for new educational methods to take into account current scientific progress, now coming into harmony with the great cultural traditions, the preservation and in-depth study of which appear essential. Unesco would be the appropriate organisation to promote such ideas.

5. The challenges of our time — the risk of destruction of our species, the impact of data processing, the implications of genetics, etc — throw a new light on the social responsibilities of the scientific community, both in the initiation and application of research. Although scientists may have no control over the applications of their discoveries, they must not remain passive when confronted with the haphazard use of what they have discovered. It is our view that the magnitude of today's challenges requires, on the one hand, a reliable and steady flow of information to the public, and, on the other hand, the establishment of multi- and transdisciplinary mechanisms for the guidance and even the carrying out of decision-making.

6. We hope that Unesco will consider this encounter as a starting point and will encourage further reflection in a spirit of transdisciplinarity and universality.

Findhorn Press is the publishing business of the Findhorn Foundation, a spiritual community in the north of Scotland. For information on visiting and participating in the life of the community and its programmes, please write to the Accommodation Secretary, Cluny Hill College, Forres, Moray, Scotland IV36 0RD.